Africa

Mary O'Keeffe

GILL EDUCATION

A map

It is a map.

I can see Africa on the map.

The sun is hot.

"This is the Sahara Desert."

It is not wet.

It is hot.

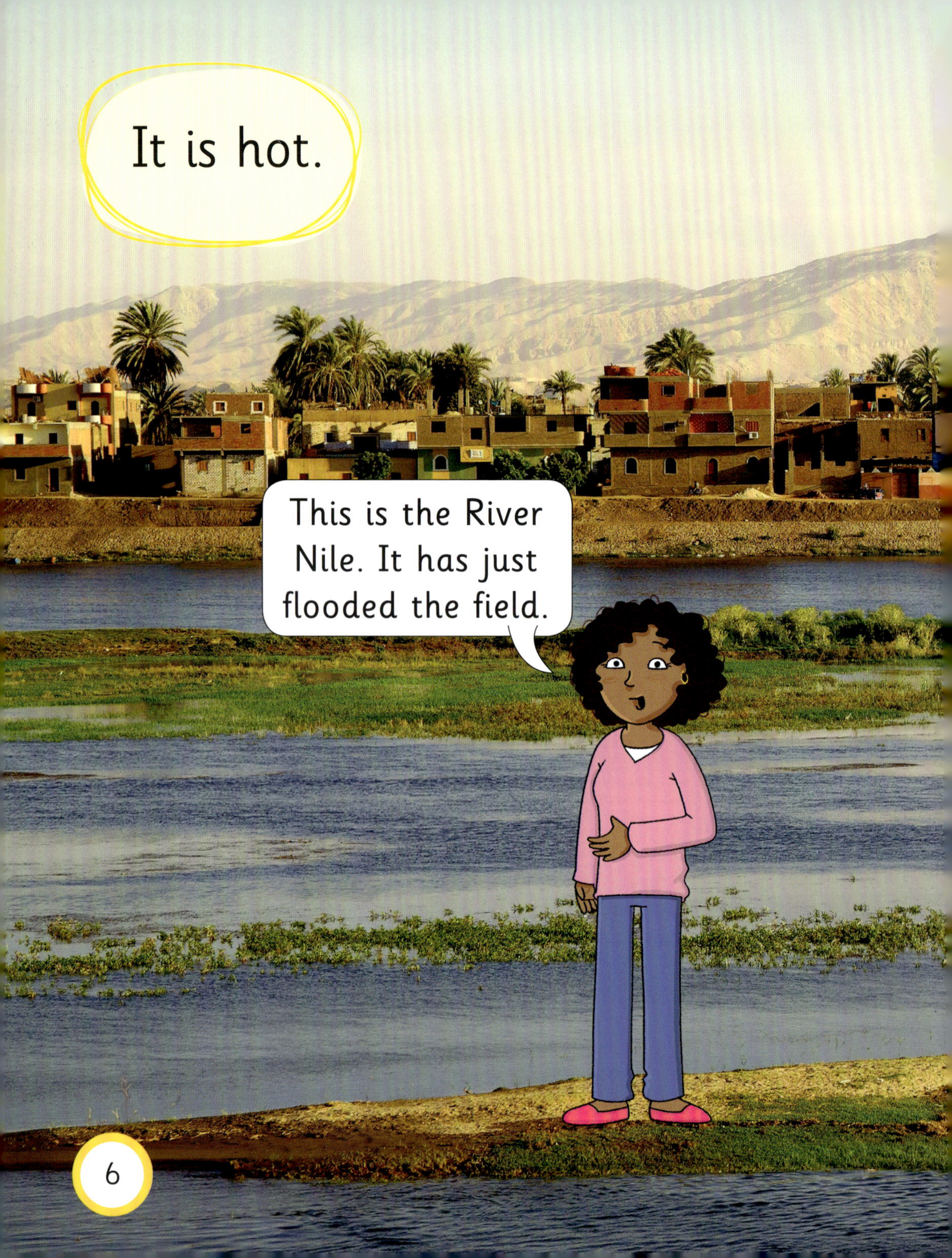

It is wet.

He is the dad.

A baby cheetah is a cub.

She is the cub.

She is big.

A baby elephant is a calf.

He is not big.

She is a wild dog.

African wild dogs are also known as painted dogs, because they have red, black, brown, white and yellow fur.

She has pups.

He is a hog.

A warthog's bumps are not really warts. They are just thick growths of skin.

He has big tusks.

It is a mix.

What animals can you see at the watering hole?

It is a big mix!